Your Flesh Shall Be A Poem
The art of plein air dance

ROBIN BISIO
FOREWARD BY ELIZABETH SCHWYZER

Images by
• ARNA BEE   • CATHERINE BENNETT   • NIK BLASKOVICH
• TOM BORTOLAZZO   • RAIZA GIORGI   • MATT KAYE
• KATHEE MILLER   • TED MILLS   • TARRL MORLEY
• BRIAN SZYMANSKI

"...and your very flesh shall be a great poem..."
Walt Whitman

I dedicate this book to my beautiful daughter Alessandra who brings the solace of love and wild things to my life.

Landé Lo in COPA DE ORO.
Photographed by Raiza Giorgi

Copyright © 2013, Robin Bisio
Photographs copyright © 2013, Arna Bee Photography: pages 7, 32,-33, 37, 46-51
Photographs copyright © 2013, Catherine Bennett: Cover, pages 8-13, 58-61
Photographs copyright © 2013, Tom Bortolazzo: pages 52-57
Photographs copyright © 2013, Raiza Giorgi: pages 3, 20-25
Photographs copyright © 2013, Matt Kaye: pages 42-45
Photographs copyright © 2013, Kathee Miller: pages 26-31, 42, 43, 45, 65
Photographs copyright © 2013, Ted Mills and Nik Blaskovich: pages 34-37
Photographs copyright © 2013, Tarrl Morley: pages 14-19, 52-57
Photographs copyright © 2013, Brian Szymanski: pages 38-41

All rights reserved.

No portion of this book may be reproduced or transmitted by any means, without written permission of the publisher, except by reviewers, who may quote brief excerpts in connection with reviews. Reviewers must request permission to use photographs, with the exception of the cover.

Published by Nauset Press

New York

info@nausetpress.com

ISBN 978-0-9851268-8-9

Please see page 62 for a complete list of exhibition and venue credits for all performances.

"Once" copyright © 1991 by Paul Celan, from *Fathomsuns and Benighted* by Paul Celan. Used by permission of Suhrkamp Verlag. Any third party use of this material outside of this publication is prohibited. Interested parties must apply directly to Suhrkamp Verlag for permission.

"Stolen Apples" copyright © 2006 by Bryant Clifford, from *The Monarch of Evening Time* by Bryant Clifford. Used by permisson of Johnny Rook Publishers. Any third party use of this material outside of this publication is prohibited. Interested parties must apply directly to Johnny Rook Publishers for permission.

"City of Moths" copyright © 2013 by Sampson Starkweather, from *The First Four Books of Sampson Starkweather* by Sampson Starkweather. Used by permisson of Birds, LLC. Any third party use of this material outside of this publication is prohibited. Interested parties must apply directly to Birds, LLC for permission.

Table of Contents

Foreward 6

Artist's Manifesto 7

Upon a Fallen Sea 8

Light Was Salvation 14

Copa de Oro 20

Picnic in Galapagos 26

Nymphaea 32

Bees Circling Heaven 38

Divination By Flight 42

Murder of Crows 46

Reign of Dreams 52

The Last Solitude 58

Credits 62

Bibliography 64

Acknowledgements 65

Foreward

SENSUAL COLLAGES: ROBIN BISIO'S DANCE LANDSCAPES

On California's south coast, sea cliffs plunge from the golden hills down to the Pacific Ocean. It's here, perched on the edge of the continent, that Robin Bisio creates her dances. For this independent choreographer and filmmaker, dance is always a response to nature: to the windswept beaches, flower-studded fields, and lush gardens of her chosen home.

Both Bisio's films and her plein air performances retain a wildness, as if the elements have shaped the work as much as the human hand. To some degree, that's true; the artist and her dancers craft each work through a collaborative process in which nature is a player. Even works begun in the studio take their cues from flora, fauna, landscape, and weather: a stag drinking from a spring, a leaf blown by the wind, a spider navigating its web. Much as a collage artist gathers and sorts her materials before choosing a final arrangement, so Bisio comes to the choreographic process with a collection of images, texts, and movement phrases. Hers is no random or purely improvisational process; the choreographer and performers are fellow translators of nature's messages.

Like her choreographic predecessor and fellow California native Isadora Duncan, Bisio celebrates the female body and its connection to the earth: bare feet and exposed skin put her dancers in direct contact with the natural world. Duncan often took her cues from classical sculpture, and so does Bisio, though she's just as likely to find inspiration in the erotic art of ancient India or the life cycle of the honeybee as in the outthrust hip of an urn-bearing maenad. Feminine sensuality is an ever-present theme.

Though the tutu is among Bisio's signature costumes and her dancers tend to be classically trained, her idiom draws upon such diverse traditions as Japanese Butoh, contact improvisation, and release technique as well as classical ballet. Her dancers roll through the grass, clamber through tidepools, and blow invisible seedpods into the breeze. Sometimes they carry bare branches; sometimes their hair is festooned with feathers; always, they interact with the landscape.

Bisio's distinct artistic vision and her sensitivity to the natural environment place her in a lineage of site-specific dance and experimental film. The same interplay between natural wildness and artful cultivation fueled the work of Maya Deren, the Ukrainian-born actress turned pioneer dance filmmaker. Deren chose southern California as her

Artist's Manifesto

adopted home and the setting for her experimental films, which like Bisio's dances feature the female figure and symbols from nature in shifting, surreal dreamscapes. Deren's silent shorts *A Study in Choreography for Camera* (1943) and *At Land* (1944) are early examples of site-specific dance captured in moving pictures: dancers tiptoe through riverbeds, roll in the surf, and leap from rock to rock in these precursors to Bisio's dance films.

For Bisio, collaborating with contemporary digital filmmakers offers yet another angle on dance: an opportunity to layer bodies and landscapes in sensual collages where canyon and creek, coastline and meadow meet and merge. Whether she sets her dancers in the stately, ornamental gardens of Montecito's Ganna Walska Lotusland or on the rugged, rock-strewn beach that lies just a short walk from her studio, Bisio is setting a stage that's at once specific and symbolic: creating dances and dance films that celebrate the landscape and point beyond it, to the timeless, evolving dance between art and nature.

—Elizabeth Schwyzer
Santa Barbara, California, June 2013

I live on the coast & this influences everything I do in dance & film-shifting, changing landscapes daily inform my stance & attitudes towards art. All is possible, all is given, all is subject to change. What is the story in why & how we alight for our time dancing on the green Earth? I am a land & sea dancer. I consider the audience to be as much the ground I walk on as the people watching.

—Robin Bisio
Santa Barbara, California, April 2012

Upon a Fallen Sea

IMAGES BY CINEMATOGRAPHER CATHERINE BENNETT

A significant collaboration with Catherine Bennett, Monica Ford, Anaya Cullen, and Dick Dunlap has helped me manifest and make concrete a film that has been in my imagination and psyche for years. It is gratifying that all of the attendant talents and insights helped it emerge into the world.

    I live in Santa Barbara, California, across the street from the wondrous cliffs of Thousand Steps Beach; they are an endless playground and source of inspiration for me. In this new work, we follow the lines of the cliffs, honoring fallen rocks and lichen with movement. Like a Chinese landscape drawing, the film will stand as a meditation on time passing, as well as a tribute to a beautiful place called home.

Light Was Salvation

IMAGES BY CINEMATOGRAPHER TARRL MORLEY

Cinematographer Tarrl Morley was in town for a week with little notice. Dorrie Tames Powell agreed to film in some favorite sweet spots—Santa Ynez River, Thousand Steps Beach—and on windswept dunes up the Central Coast by Pismo. We went with little set choreography, letting nature have her way on the dance. The resulting film, *Light Was Salvation*, has wind and sparkles on water as co-conspirators.

It was a bucolic spring week except for the day on the dunes when it was so cold that Dorrie's daughter Aiyana and I huddled in a shelter wrapped in our checkered picnic blanket. I periodically ran out to give somewhat directorial instructions to Tarrl and Dorrie in a perfect storm of sand. "Keep falling," I said to Dorrie as she rolled down the dunes. We had to get the camera cleaned out at a camera shop when we stopped for lunch.

ONCE
I heard him,
he was washing the
world,
unseen, nightlong,
real.

One and Infinite,
annihilated,
ied.

Light was. Salvation.

—Paul Celan

We spent a day on the Santa Ynez River, with Dorrie floating and swimming in the not-so-warm water, all the while ignoring the catcalls of boys visiting Red Rock to jump into the river from a nearby cliff face. I also remember stopping traffic with impunity on the little road that ran through the water when we were filming Dorrie in the reeds. The resulting film looks peaceful and inevitable, as if to belie any stress in its making.

Copa de Oro

PHOTOGRAPHED BY RAIZA GIORGI

We shot *Copa de Oro* at Nojoqui Falls Ranch, with Raiza Giorgi at the helm of both camera and all-terrain vehicle. The stunning dancer Landé Lo wore a gorgeous dress by Anaya Cullen. Ted Mills was our director, with Nik Blaskovich as cinematographer. Ted and Nik were going for a look that captured an Old West feel, with fixed shots taken from a distance to capture the whole vivid panorama. My job on set was to adjust the choreography to avoid rocks, snakes, and cow pies. It is not easy to dance on uneven terrain, but Landé was heroic: a wildebeest turned mythic dancer.

We stopped for a lovely midday picnic, and friends came out to join us. It was a family affair on an old California rancho, and we had a blast barreling over the hills on ATVs to each new location!

Landé's dress dazzled in the high noon light. She matched the color of the lichens on the rocks and the iconic California poppy. As she leaped through the chaparral, she was springtime, personified.

IN THE POPPY FIELD

Mad Patsy said, he said to me,
That every morning he could see
An angel walking on the sky;
Across the sunny skies of morn
He threw great handfuls far and nigh
Of poppy seed among the corn;
And then, he said, the angels run
To see the poppies in the sun.

A poppy is a devil weed,
I said to him-he disagreed;
He said the devil had no hand
In spreading flowers tall and fair
Through corn and rye and meadow land,
by garth and barrow everywhere:
The devil has not any flower,
But only money in his power.

And then he stretched out in the sun
And rolled upon his back for fun:
He kicked his legs and roared for joy
Because the sun was shining down:
He said he was a little boy
And would not work for any clown:
He ran and laughed behind a bee,
And danced for very ecstasy.

—James Stephens

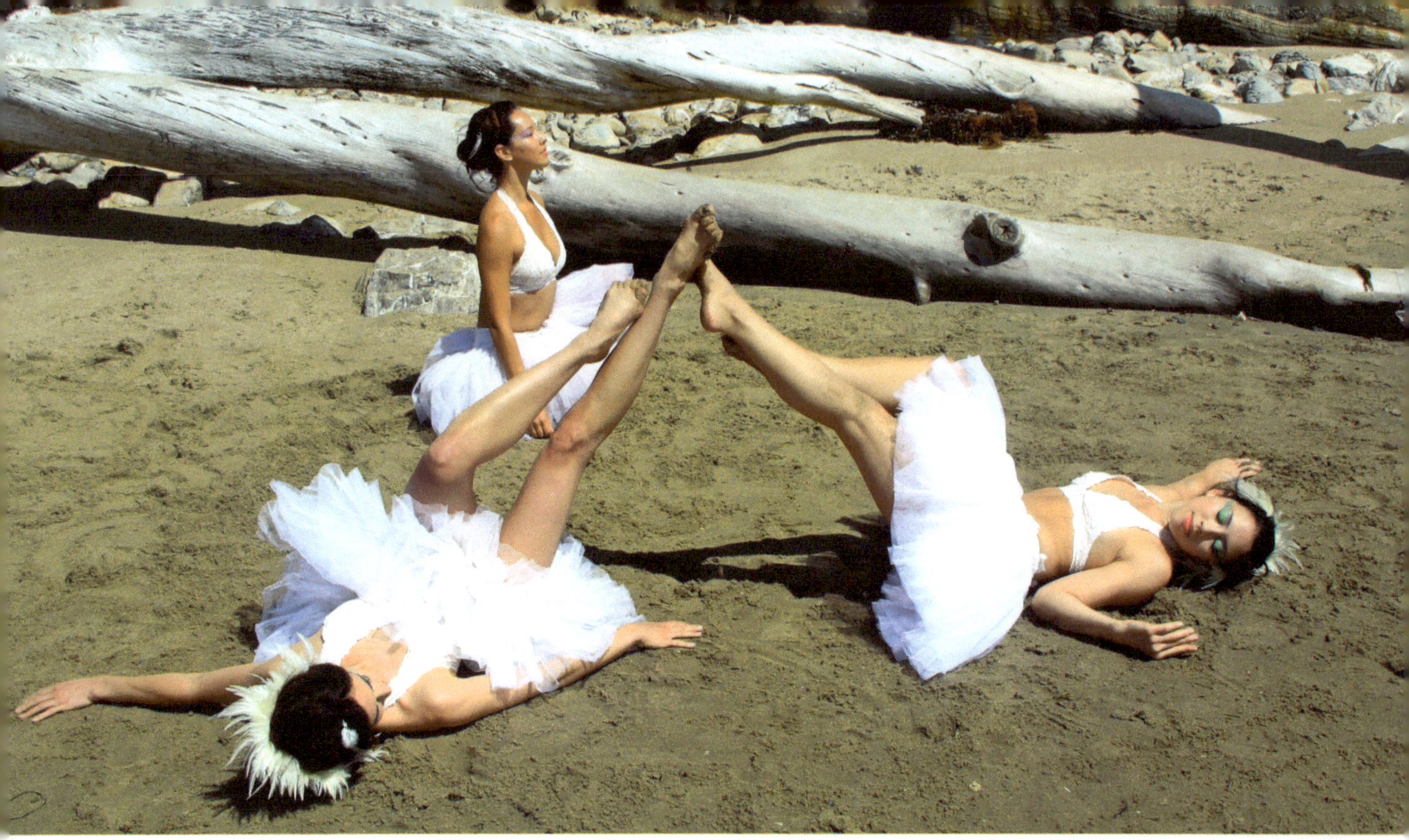

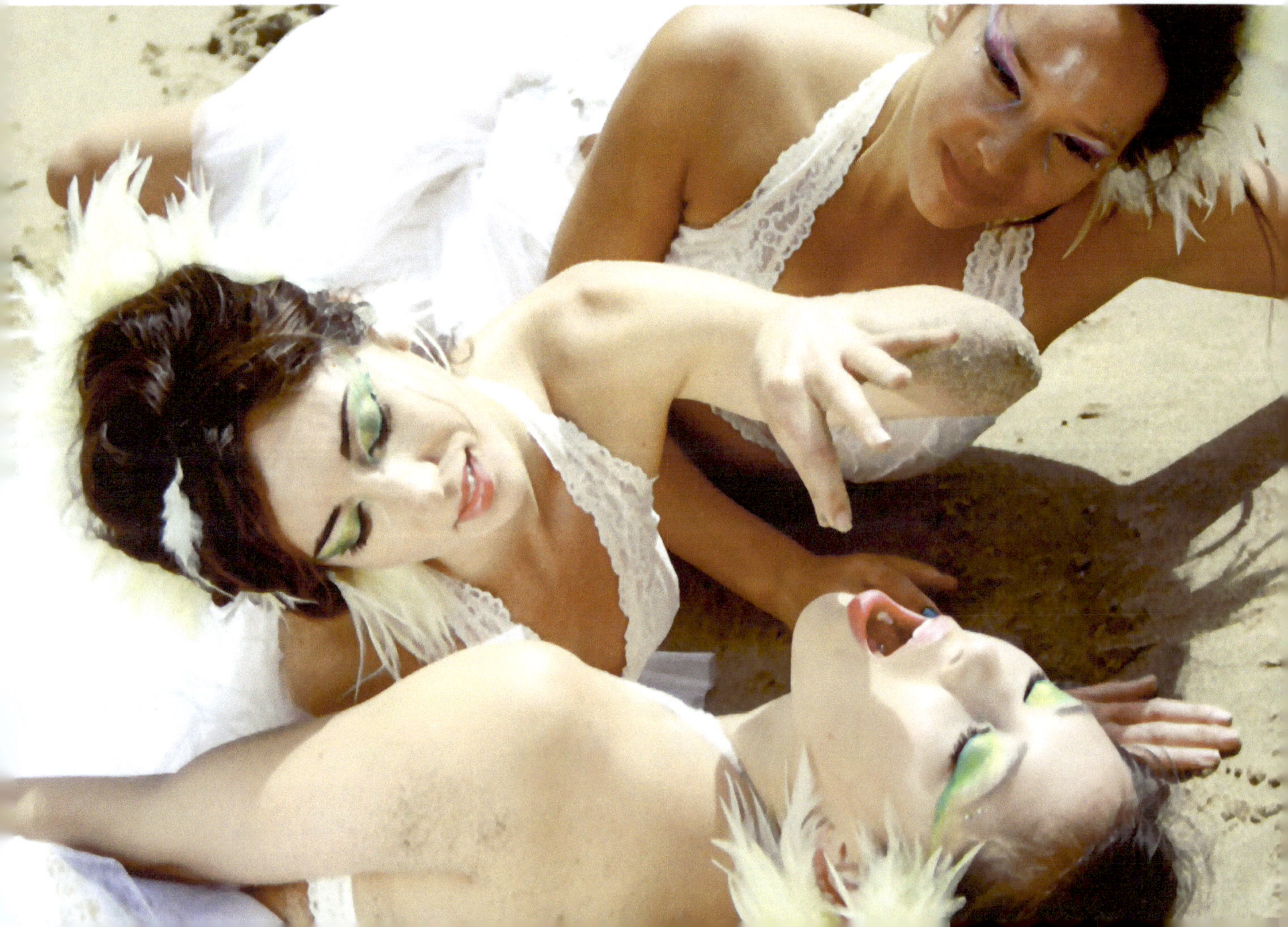

PHOTOGRAPHED BY KATHEE MILLER

Picnic in Galapagos is an homage to my adventurous daughter Ally, who spent nearly a month there during her senior year in high school. She volunteered on a farm, cutting back invasive blackberry bushes with machetes during a four day week and was free to travel around the islands during her time off. I got rapturous if sporadic reports from Ally of swimming in the sea surrounded by shiny fish as far as the eye could see, riding the waves with surfing iguanas, sailing past islands populated by pink flamingos, watching giant tortoises mate, and being surrounded by seals as she sat on a rock, eating an ice cream cone. She was also on a boat that took on water and almost sunk; apparently this happens a lot. Luckily they were near a port and switched to another boat!

We filmed *Picnic in Galapagos* with dancers Bonnie Crotzer, Monica Ford, and Kaita Lepore Mrazek at a Santa Barbara beach. Clad in Anaya Cullen's feathery, white costumes, the dancers seem like denizens of those faraway shores.

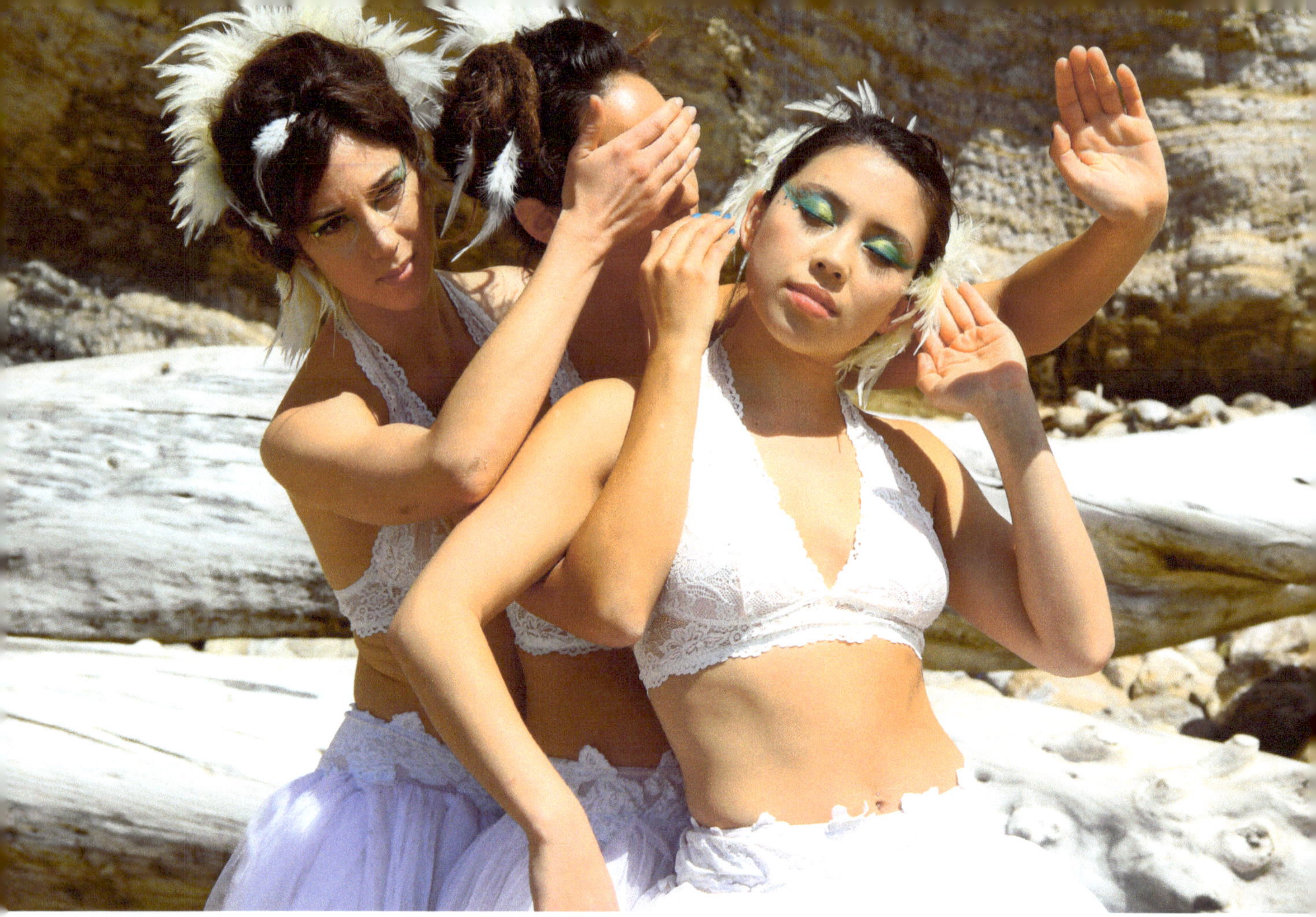

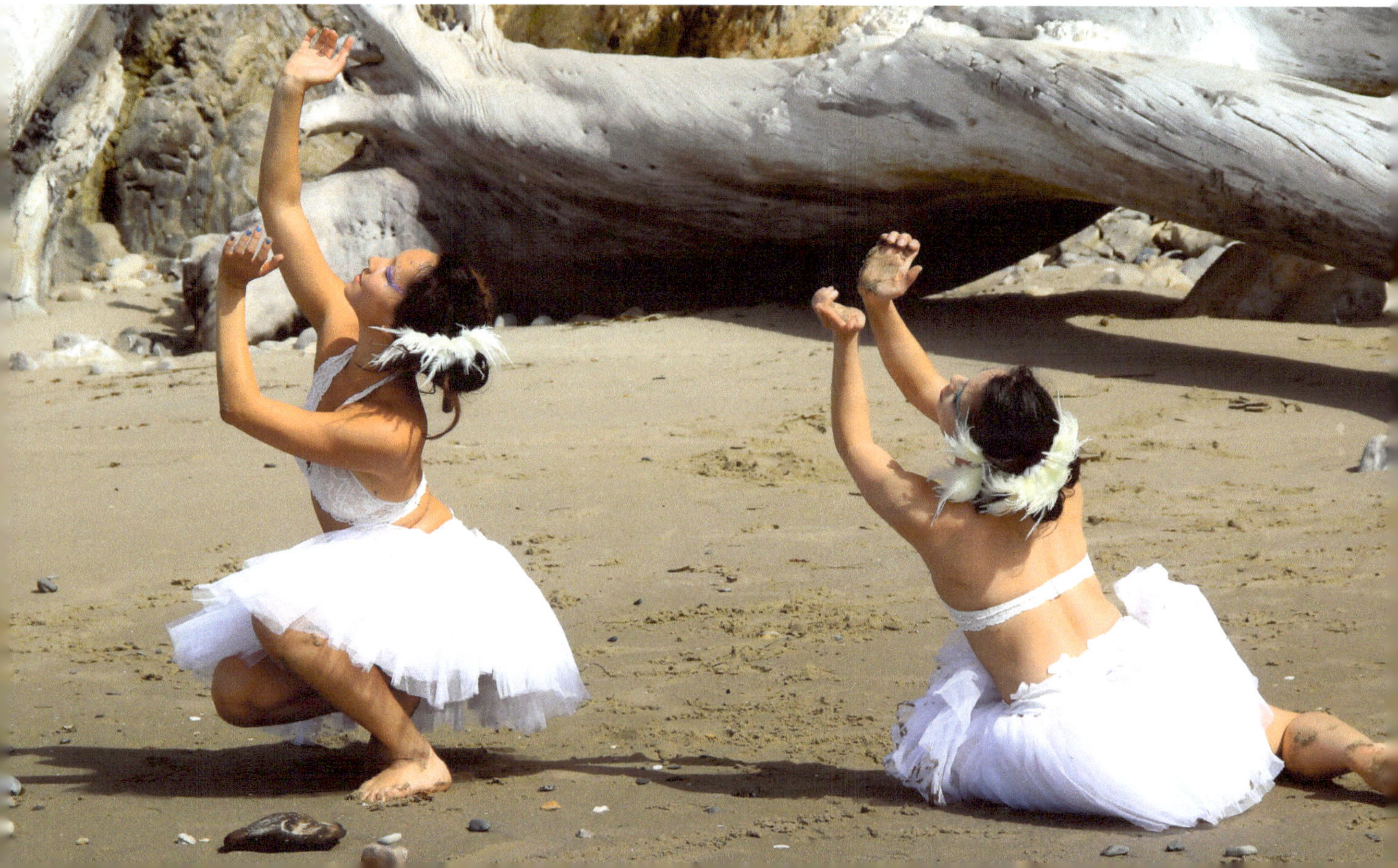

STOLEN APPLE

Table of Contents...

Chapter 1..On a bed of pine needles

2...My skirt of mint leaves open

3..Her poison oak curse

4..On his bare chested rock lover

5...Friend of the sea lion-

Our book was stolen

for the subaqueous library of blue lineage,

written for us, in our language;

scrolled from the feather of a seagull,

scratched on a kelp bed,

one hundred feet below sea level.

-Bryant Clifford

Nymphaea

PHOTOGRAPHS BY ARNA BEE PHOTOGRAPHY
IMAGES BY CINEMATOGRAPHER NIK BLASKOVICH WITH DIRECTOR TED MILLS

Here is dancer Erika Kloumann at fabled Ganna Walska Lotusland in *Nymphaea*, a dance I choreographed for an installation that was presented as part of the Santa Barbara International Film Festival. Ted Mills and Nik Blaskovich filmed Erika and the garden to appear as a triptych on curved screens–this in homage to the Jeu de Paume in Paris where Monet's waterlilies are on display.

Nymphaea speaks to the heart of the giant pink lotus flowers that open in full majestic bloom at Ganna Walska's glorious Lotus Pond come summer. It speaks, too, to the iridescent Abalone Pool. And to the giant wash of green of the Great Lawn. And the most mysterious Japanese Garden with shrines and ginkgo trees hiding the fortunes of true bloom. As Erika Kloumann romps through Lotusland, it is clear that creativity itself is alive and well in this enchanted place.

from ODE ON A GRECIAN URN

Thou still unravish'd bride of quietness,
Thou foster-child of Silence and slow Time,
Sylvan historian, who canst thus express
   A flowery tale more sweetly than our rhyme:
What leaf-fringed legend haunts about thy shape
   Of deities or mortals, or of both,
     In Tempe or the dales of Arcady?
What men or gods are these? What maidens loth?
What mad pursuit? What struggle to escape?
What pipes and timbrels? What wild ecstasy?

                                    - John Keats

Bees Circling Heaven

IMAGES BY CINEMATOGRAPHER BRIAN SZYMANSKI

Drawing on the rich tradition of Indian miniature paintings, *Bees Circling Heaven* speaks to the erotic impulse of goddess energy–a kind of earth pollination of feminine spirit. The dance also references Bhramari Devi, the Indian goddess of the black bees and protector of the heart chakra. With movement in turn yielding, provocative, and strong, Bonnie Crotzer is a vortex of the divine return. The gardens at Lotusland are the perfect place for a goddess bee to alight.

from THE BEE'S SONG

Do not tie my wings,
Says the honey-bee;
Do not bind my wings,
Leave them glad and free.
If I fly abroad,
If I keep afar,
Humming all the day,
Where wild blossoms are,
'Tis to bring you sweets,
Rich as summer joy,
Clear--as gold and glass;
The divinest toy
That the god's have left,
Is the pretty hive,
Where a maiden reigns,
And the busy thrive.

If you bar my way,
Your delight is gone,
No more honey-gems;
From the heather borne;
No more tiny thefts,
From your neighbor's rose,
Who were glad to guess
Where its sweetness goes.

Let the man of arts
Ply his plane and glass;
Let the vapors rise,
Let the liquor pass;
...

...
Not the task of both
Such a treasure yields;
Honey, Pan ordained,
Food for gods and men,
Only in my way
Shall you store again.
Leave me to my will

While the bright days glow,
While the sleepy flowers
Quicken as I go.
When the pretty ones
Look to me no more,
Dead, beneath your feet,
Crushed and dabbled o'er;
In my narrow cell
I will fold my wing;
Sink in dark and chill,
A forgotten thing.

Can you read the song
Of the suppliant bee?
'Tis a poet's soul,
Asking liberty.

-Julia Ward Howe

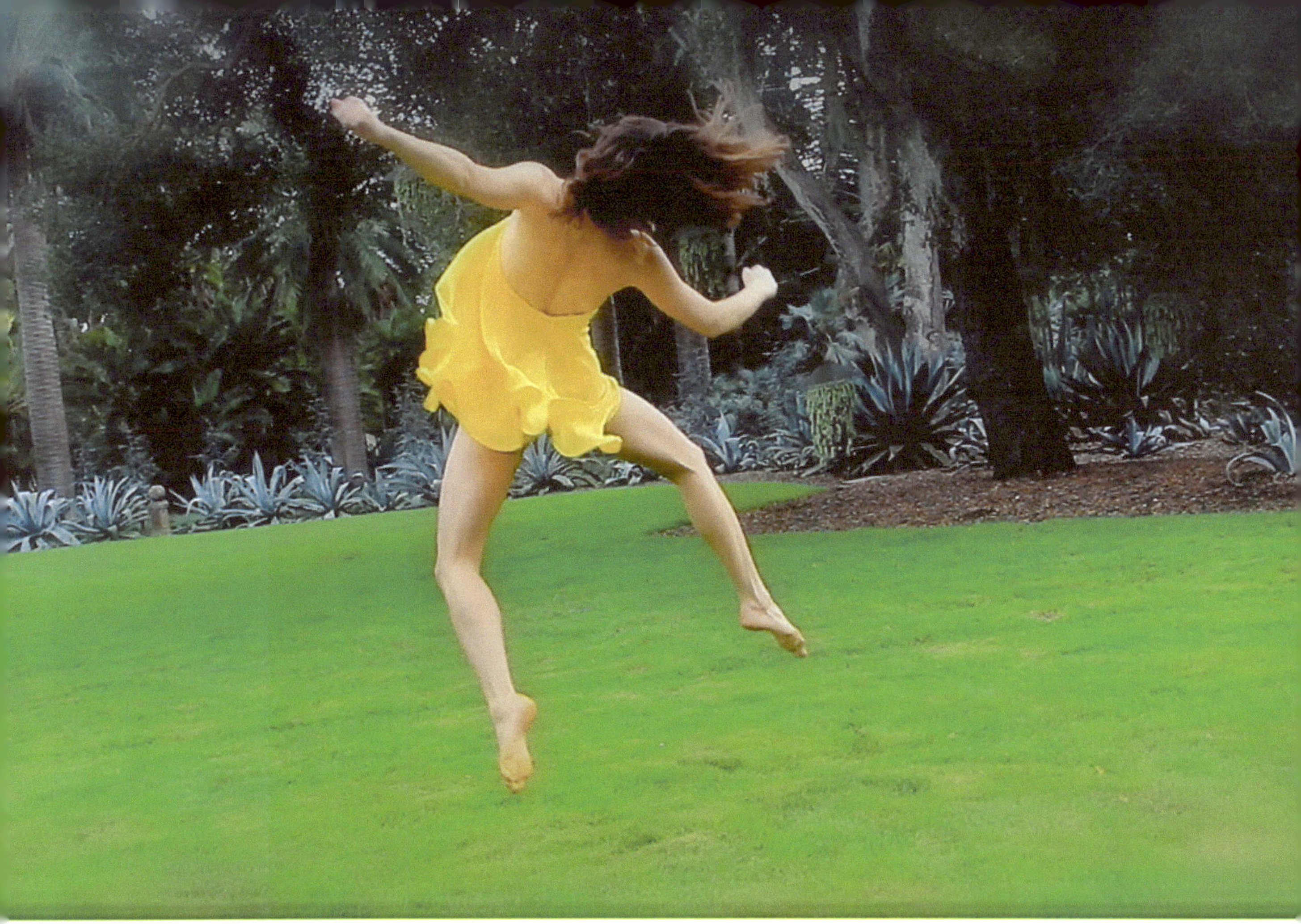

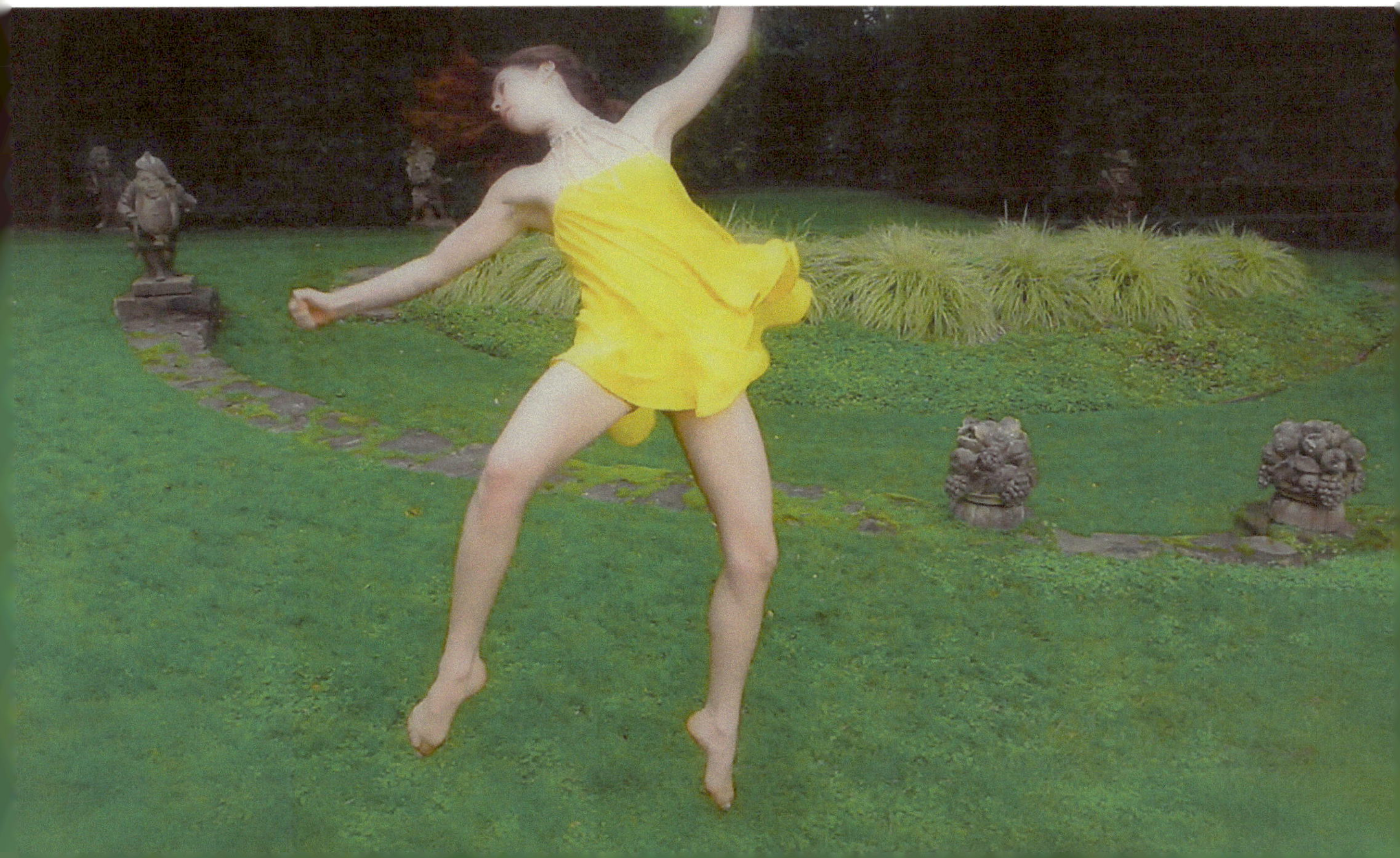

Divination by Flight

PHOTOGRAPHED BY MATT KAYE AND KATHEE MILLER

They touched down for a short time on the fallen tree altars at Mesa Lane Beach, these dancers of beauty and drama. The story is as old as time. What do the flights of birds tell us of destiny? Dancers Leila Drake Fossek and Alyson Mattoon are best friends. I think you can read their alchemy of delight as they dance around reflective tidepools, more avian than human. This is where life becomes myth.

THE FLIGHT

Look back with longing eyes and know that I will follow,
Lift me up in your love as a light wind lifts a swallow,
Let our flight be far in sun or windy rain-
But what if I heard my first love calling me again?

Hold me on your heart as the brave sea holds the foam,
Take me far away to the hills that hide your home;
Peace shall thatch the roof and love shall latch the door-

But what if I heard my first love calling me once more?

-Sara Teasdale

Murder of Crows

IMAGES BY CINEMATOGRAPHER ARNA BEE

Murder of Crows is a day in the life of a winged dancer who haunts the cliffs, fields, and rocky outcroppings of Lizard's Mouth, a ridge of sandstone in the Santa Ynez Mountains overlooking Santa Barbara. The dance is at once a lament and a prayer to the mountain gods. In her nest of sky, the dancer orchestrates a waltz of mist and a theology of clouds. A location above the treeline evokes beauty and mystery. It was a winter day of wildness, the cupped hand of nature herself blessing the filming by keeping dancer Kaita Lepore Mrazek warm and the camera dry. It was the kind of day I long for and dream about and then, through photography and film editing, such a day emerges out of time, emblematic of our sojourn here on earth.

from A MASK PRESENTED
AT LUDLOW CASTLE, 1634
And Wisdoms self
Oft seeks to sweet retired Solitude,
Where with her best nurse Contemplation
She plumes her feathers, and lets grow her wings
That in the various bussle of resort
Were all to ruffl'd, and somtimes impair'd.

-John Milton

Reign of Dreams
at the Guadalupe Dunes

PHOTOGRAPHED BY TOM BORTOLAZZO WITH
IMAGES BY CINEMATOGRAPHER TARRL MORLEY

Early in the morning, we drove to costume designer Marlene Mason's childhood home in Lompoc. In the rec room, we commenced the painstaking process of painting the dancers white with a pigment designed by Marlene; it was a very exotic blend. Emboldened by the body paint and fortified with coffee, we trekked one mile until we reached the dunes themselves, traversing streams and crossing a long, wooden boardwalk over exotic marshlands. No one was in sight the whole time. It was windy and freezing and gloriously blue. The dancers looked stunning in white against the blue sky and pale dunes. Our cinematographer Tarrl Morley was having none of it. He was shooting 16mm black-and-white with a hand-held red filter over the lens to give the proceedings an eerie, otherworldly feeling.

Each dancer had a makeup artist to replenish the shimmering but delicate white paint. Adrianne Davis, who had obviously been on a lot of sets, rushed to cover the dancers with jackets after every take. It felt like we were on the moon, or at least in prehistoric California, with long, unfettered beach views. This is where Cecil B. DeMille filmed *The Ten Commandments*, the site was very inspiring. We had only scouted briefly. The day of the shoot we found places to film as we were hiking in: 'Hey, how about that dune?' and 'Yes, that inland sea.'

The dancers were troupers. They became inhabitants of a place out of time.

In addition to making a film of *Reign of Dreams* and a Lobero Theater performance with the Santa Barbara Dance Alliance, we also presented the dance at the Pacific Ocean, on the beach at Thousand Steps. I ordered fragrant plumeria leis for the dancers from my favorite shop in Honolulu–Cindy's in Chinatown–and had them shipped over. After all, I created this dance in Kauai while visiting my honorary tutu, or grandmother. I think of this dance as a gift from across the Pacific Ocean.

I wrote this poem as part of a dance score I created for my longtime collaborator and dancer, Cybil Gilbertson. She has spent spent a lot of time in Hawaii and has much aloha.

—Robin Bisio

FOR CYBIL

chimera
lock and embrace of the
unknown world
picked bamboo
a monk seal digesting
sit down to hula on secret beach
levitate, ginger in the hills
attitude back, open for the unexpected
sharks, hurricanes, tidal waves
finger trail down chakras to restless sea
third eye reduced to basics
white orchid, lost language
all the lava, ancient fire
at the lagoon kiss into hand
to guard the light
spin like the moon is eating you
fly with ear
wind at night, sleep and dream in
seagrass constellations
legs trail in back, comet
keep running
light and dark are connected,
a breath away
stand on toes, twist
how peaceful starlight is
blow into partner's heart
push up, change, collapse on roots of sheltering tree
hand on toe like mountain
but Buddha in cellular embrace

map of hidden coconuts, man o ray
still life without artificial excitement
jumping jack
collapse on self, shake all over like wave
slow dance like the breeze
letting go of old ways
moon dip, a cup of jasmine tea
sarongs on the line
endlessly seductive
pattern on water
pattern under water
strong against the current
early rain in mouth
cardinal's cry, bitter rain
of spinner dolphins and centipedes

how do prayers
reside in landscapes?
the trades are down
there's a sweet wind in the hammock
heat is rising over grass
with the deep blue of a hidden past
don't lose the path
between the infinite and the known, gallop
arms cross and fall out of each other
in the church of shells,
form follows function
(Anahola, Kauai)

—Robin Bisio

The Last Solitude

IMAGES BY CINEMATOGRAPHER CATHERINE BENNETT

Sand and sea are a natural stage for Erika Kloumann. When Catherine Bennett and I filmed her at the beach in *The Last Solitude*, it seemed as if Erika inhabited the seashore. If mermaids are real, she is proof indeed. Wet and cold on the sand, she jumped high amid rocks and spun into encroaching tides.

 We premiered *The Last Solitude* at the Santa Barbara International Film Festival. Catherine had the brilliant idea to project the film on a giant hand-crafted block of ice. We somehow got permission for all the lights to be turned off at the Santa Barbara County Courthouse, where we presented our installation under the arched entryway. How mysterious on a winter night to approach a major Santa Barbara edifice in total darkness with this film as a a beacon, seeming to emanate from the glowing, dripping ice.

from CITY OF MOTHS

The sea again? The problem is she is also afraid of the future. Whose condition shares the characters of water. We are animals of the conditional. We float belly-up. Streams and rivers flow forward, but not the sea. You see my dilemma? I wouldn't lie to you. Despite how excited she gets, she will always stop at the first sign of sand. Goddess of giving way. It's not the idea of the future, to reach the other side of desire–it is simply her lot. But you never know, maybe someday even the sea will flow forward.

–Sampson Starkweather

Credits

UPON A FALLEN SEA, pages 8-13
A film by Catherine Bennett and Robin Bisio.
Choreography and Co-Director: ROBIN BISIO
Cinematographer, Editor and Co-Director: CATHERINE BENNETT
Dancer: MONICA FORD
Music: DICK DUNLAP
Costume Design and Styling: ANAYA CULLEN
Film Stills: CATHERINE BENNETT
Filmed on location at Leadbetter Beach, Santa Barbara, Ca.

LIGHT WAS SALVATION, pages 14-19
A film by Robin Bisio and Tarrl Morley.
Director: ROBIN BISIO
Choreography: ROBIN BISIO and DORRIE TAMES POWELL
Cinematographer and Editor: TARRL MORLEY
Score: TARRL MORLEY
Dancer: DORRIE TAMES POWELL
Costume Design: MARLENE MASON
Film Stills: TARRL MORLEY
Filmed on location at Thousand Steps Beach, Pismo Dunes, and Santa Ynez River, Ca.

COPA DE ORO, pages 20-25
A film by Nik Blaskovich, Robin Bisio, Anaya Cullen and Ted Mills
Choreography: ROBIN BISIO
Director: TED MILLS
Cinematographer: NIK BLASKOVICH
Editor: ARNA BEE
Dancer: LANDÉ LO
Costume design and Styling: ANAYA CULLEN
Photo Credit: RAIZA GIORGI
Shot on location at Nojoqui Falls Ranch, Santa Barbara County, Ca.

PICNIC IN GALAPAGOS, pages 26-31
A dance by Robin Bisio.
Choreographer: ROBIN BISIO
Dancers: BONNIE CROTZER, MONICA FORD, CYBIL GILBERTSON and KAITA LEPORE MRAZEK
Costume Design and Styling: ANAYA CULLEN
Music For Stage: GHOST TIGER
Photo Credit: KATHEE MILLER
Shot on location at Mesa Lane Beach, Santa Barbara, Ca.

NYMPHAEA, pages 32-37
A film by Nik Blaskovich, Robin Bisio and Ted Mills.
Choreography: ROBIN BISIO
Director and Editor: TED MILLS
Cinematographer: NIK BLASKOVICH
Score: TED MILLS
Dancer: ERIKA KLOUMANN
Costume Design: JEN SANTAROSSA
Styling: KELSEY BODINE
Installation design: JONATHAN SMITH
Photo Credit: ARNA BEE; Film Stills: NIK BLASKOVICH and TED MILLS
Film designed as a multi-screen installation for the Santa Barbara International Film Festival
Filmed on location at Ganna Walska Lotusland, Montecito, Ca.

BEES CIRCLING HEAVEN, pages 32-35
A dance and film by Robin Bisio.
Choreography and Director: ROBIN BISIO
Cinematographer and Editor: BRIAN SZYMANSKI
Costume Design and Styling: ANAYA CULLEN
Dancers: BONNIE CROTZER, WESLIE CHING,
MONICA FORD, and KAITA LEPORE MRAZEK
Music: GHOST TIGER
Film Stills: BRIAN SZYMANSKI
Performance and film for Swarm at Ganna Walska Lotusland and the Vita Apis Collective
Filmed on location at Ganna Walska Lotusland, Montecito, Ca.

DIVINATION BY FLIGHT, pages 36-41
A dance by Robin Bisio.
Choreographer: ROBIN BISIO
Dancers: LEILA DRAKE FOSSEK, CYBIL GILBERTSON, ALYSON MATTOON,
SARAH PON, and MELISSA ULLOM
Costumes: ROBIN BISIO
Photo Credit: MATT KAYE and KATHEE MILLER
Shot on location at Mesa Lane Beach, Santa Barbara, Ca.

MURDER OF CROWS, pages 42-47
A film by Robin Bisio and Arna Bee.
Choreographer and Director: ROBIN BISIO
Cinematographer and Editor: ARNA BEE
Music: JEN BARON
Dancer: KAITA LEPORE MRAZEK
Costume Design and Styling: KAITA LEPORE MRAZEK
Film Stills: ARNA BEE
Filmed on location at Lizard's Mouth, Santa Barbara County, Ca.

REIGN OF DREAMS, pages 48-53
A dance and film by Robin Bisio.
Choreography and Director: ROBIN BISIO
Cinematographer: TARRL MORLEY
Editor: CHARLENE HUSTON
Dancers: CYBIL GILBERTSON, ERIKA KLOUMANN and LEXI PEARL
Costume Design and Styling: MARLENE MASON
Music: DICK DUNLAP
Photo credit: TOM BORTOLAZZO Film Stills: TARRL MORLEY
Shot on location at Guadalupe Dunes, Santa Barbara County, Ca. and Thousand Steps Beach, Santa Barbara, Ca.

THE LAST SOLITUDE, pages 54-59
A film by Catherine Bennett and Robin Bisio.
Choreography and Co-Director: ROBIN BISIO
Cinematographer, Editor and Co-Director: CATHERINE BENNETT
Dancer: ERIKA KLOUMANN
Film Stills: CATHERINE BENNETT
Film designed for ice projection and installation for the
Santa Barbara International Film Festival
Filmed on location at Thousand Steps Beach, Santa Barbara, Ca.

Bibliography

Celan, Paul. "Once." *Fathomsuns and Benighted*. Trans. Ian Fairley. Manchester: Carcanet Press, 1991. Print.

Clifford, Bryant. "Stolen Apples." *The Monarch of Evening Time*. Carmel: Johnny Rook Publishers, 2006. Print.

Howe, Julia Ward. "The Bee's Song." *Poemhunter.com*. Web. June 2013.

Keats, John. "Ode on a Grecian Urn." *Poemhunter.com*. Web. July 2013.

Milton, John. "A Mask Presented at Ludlow Castle, 1634." *The Milton Reading Room*. Ed. Luxon, Thomas H. Web. July 2013. <http://dartmouth.edu/~milton>

Shakespeare, William. "The Winter's Tale." *The Oxford Shakespeare*. Ed. Craig, W.J. London: Oxford University Press, 1914. New York: Bartleby.com, 2000. Web. July 2013.

Starkweather, Sampson. "City of Moths." *The First Four Books of Sampson Starkweather*. Austin, Minneapolis, New York, Raleigh: Birds, LLC, 2013. Print.

Stephens, James. "In The Poppy Fields." *Poemhunter.com*. Web. July 2013.

Teasdale, Sara. "The Flight." *Poemhunter.com*. Web. July 2013.

A note on the type used in this book:
Body type is Fragment Core, by Shuji Kikuchi, dafont.com
Italics are 2011 Slimtype by Gilles Le Corre, myfonts.com
Bylines are Paris, by La Goupil Paris, myfonts.com
Handwriting is Jellyka St. Andrew's Queen, by Jellyka Nerevan, cuttyfruty.com

DIVINATION BY FLIGHT
Photographed by Kathee Miller

Acknowledgements

Creating a dance (and in this case, a book) is an intensely collaborative art. Without each and every person who contributed to the larger picture, something essential would be missing. Many thanks to the *Dancers*: Monica Ford, Dorrie Tames Powell, Landé Lo, Erika Kloumann, Bonnie Crotzer, Cybil Gilbertson, Kaita Lepore Mrazek, Weslie Ching, Leila Drake Fossek, Alyson Mattoon, Sarah Pon, Melissa Ullom, Lexi Pearl; *Stylists* and *Costume Designers*: Anaya Cullen, Kelsey Bodine, Marlene Mason, Jen Santarossa; *Musicians*: Dick Dunlap, Jen Baron, Ghost Tiger; and other *Contributors*: Jonathan Smith, Charlene Huston. Special appreciation and thanks to the *Photographers*: Raiza Giorgi, Matt Kaye, Kathee Miller, Tom Bortolazzo; and *Cinematographers*: Catherine Bennett, Arna Bee, Brian Szymanski, Tarrl Morley, Nik Blaskovich, Ted Mills; all whom provided stunning imagery and gave permission to use their work in this book. Elizabeth Schwyzer provided valuable writing and editing skills. Anna Moser of Suhrkamp Verlag kindly gave us permission to reprint Paul Celan's *Once*. Karyn Kloumann of Nauset Press brought the book to fruition. And the *Poets*: Bryant Clifford, Sampson Starkweather, Paul Celan, Julia Ward Howe, Sara Teasdale, James Stephens, William Shakespeare, John Keats, John Milton; whose words, included in this book, provided me with the sparks of inspiration that-fueled and tended by many-became dances. Heartfelt gratitude to all.

www.ingramcontent.com/pod-product-compliance
Lightning Source LLC
Chambersburg PA
CBHW042019150426
43197CB00002B/74